C000254293

Cover: Neverending views from the Pewsey Downs

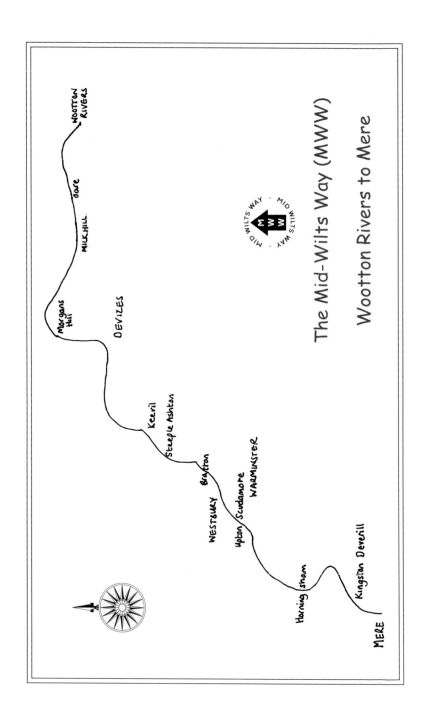

The Mid-Wilts Way (MWW)

Wootton Rivers to Mere

The Mid-Wilts Way

*A 55-mile walk across Wiltshire
from Wootton Rivers in the east
to Mere in the south-west*

James Alsop

EX LIBRIS PRESS

Published in 2007 by
EX LIBRIS PRESS
16A St John's Road
St Helier
Jersey   JE2 3LD

Origination by Ex Libris Press

Printed by Cromwell Press
Trowbridge, Wiltshire

© 2007 James Alsop

ISBN 978-1-903341-42-1

*To Kate, Evangeline and Isabella,
three very special girls*

Mixed Sources
Product group from well-managed
forests and other controlled sources
www.fsc.org Cert no. TT-TOC-2082
© 1996 Forest Stewardship Council
FSC

Contents

Walkers tackling the steepest ascent of the Mid-Wilts Way where the route rejoins the Pewsey Downs to the west of Oare

Introduction

The Mid-Wilts Way (Mid-Wiltshire Way), an elevated route over much of Wiltshire's glorious downland, represents a 55-mile walk across the county, starting in the east in the village of Wootton Rivers and ending in the south-west close to the Dorset border in the old village of Mere.

The walk is a delightful one, possessing dramatic and charming characteristics in almost equal measure. This is due to both the rural nature of Wiltshire and the lofty heights that dominate much of the route.

Further, whilst the way passes through no mountain or true upland areas, sights no ocean panoramas or lakeside settings, its diversity is outstanding. When hills are abandoned, picturesque villages replace them; so too do stretches of quiet and colour-filled countryside. A substantial section of the Kennet and Avon Canal is woven into the route; even the road and lane sections have been included for their aesthetic qualities as well as simple convenience.

Neither can one ignore the walk's historical associations. There is substantial evidence of ancient human activity, especially between the end of the Pewsey Downs and Roundway Hill, and hill-top burial grounds are encountered periodically. In addition, a number of attractive and interesting churches encountered *en route* are literally within touching distance. A few non-conformist chapels, still open, are also on or close to the Way. A diverse array of wildlife is a constant companion – hardly surprising when one notes that the route passes through a number of nature reserves and long stretches of quite remote countryside.

This walk therefore has something for everyone. Whether you wish to experience quiet villages, steep and dramatic climbs followed by long stretches of downland, far-reaching views in many shades of green, a canal-side stroll sampling our industrial heritage and modern day leisure pursuits, small sections of woodland, historic churches, plus a choice of pleasing rural accommodation and pubs – all these are available in significant measure. But, above all, it is the seemingly endless miles of unspoilt countryside, viewed from high, steep-sided hills, that gives this walk irresistible appeal.

Neverending views from the Pewsey Downs

Brief History of the Mid-Wilts Way

After many years of mainly upland walking, no doubt like many before me, I started to develop more of an interest in lowland exploration, as a distinct alternative.

My lowland experiences soon started to impress on me just how much the open countryside of southern England had to offer. For a start the climate is wonderfully generous, in stark contrast to that of upland Britain; rain is refreshing, winds often invigorate the walker rather than blast him/her off the hillside in fear, snow – if it ever falls – is a benign novelty that adds a touch of romance rather than a threat to life and, crucially, sunny and clear days are a common companion, rather than an unexpected bonus.

But this is only part of the story! When walking in the countryside the diversity on offer is often overwhelming, with hill-top views displaying a patchwork of colour and cultivation, where man, machine and the land have largely harmonised their activity. Mile after mile of supreme walking can be embarked upon with relaxed confidence notwithstanding the fright that the occasional 'Bull in the Field' sign can engender; surprisingly quiet and even remote tracts of countryside are encountered in which delightful village settlements are rarely far away. Further, once one has accepted that a rural lowland alternative is not a poor second best to the mountains, the question is raised of 'why travel considerable distances when Wiltshire is essentially a rural and, at times, hilly county, especially within the context of southern Britain?' Addressing this question opened up the opportunity to explore way beyond the confines of a few favourite, short local walks, and to ponder seriously the potential for more substantial options.

Being a lover of maps, OS maps especially, little encouragement was needed to scour the county for possible long distance walks. The Mere to Wootton Rivers itinerary jumped out at me because of the opportunity it provided to link the higher ground of Wiltshire, enjoying belvedere views for much of the way. Many times I had longingly viewed the Pewsey Downs from Westbury White Horse, but now an opportunity to link them, on one continuous walk, was a potential reality.

Following the route on the ground posed few if any problems. However it is perhaps a statement of the obvious that quietly pursuing a route on your own, with no intention of publishing the same, provides far greater freedom to walk, even where no public rights of way exist. Preparing a route for publication requires more care, planning, research and persistence.

Once the process of establishing a route suitable for publication was commenced, the setbacks only served to make it more important to see the task through. It does however raise the question as to whether or not the original qualities of the walk have been compromised in order to ensure a publishable route. In response I would simply assert that all publishable routes require a responsible attitude on behalf of the author, not just to prevent confusion, problems and conflicts, but for conscience sake. That said, alterations to the first route I optimistically followed are relatively minor, and thus the resulting walk remains a delightful one, with numerous highlights and copious opportunities for legitimate digression.

Villages on the Mid-Wilts Way

The MWW passes through no less than nine villages! Thus, on average, every six miles or so walkers will encounter a small Wiltshire settlement, adding immeasurably to their overall experience. Legitimate diversions may well detain you and, of course, the opportunity for refreshment and accommodation will often be available. This is to say nothing of many other villages and hamlets, a little off the Way, whose charms may lure you into straying from the route.

Bearing these thoughts in mind, listed below are the nine villages through which the Way passes, in east-to-west order, together with a few brief comments about each.

Wootton Rivers
A stunning start (or finish) point deep in the heart of rural eastern Wiltshire, where picturesque thatched cottages draw the eye and where accommodation and sustenance is available at the Royal Oak inn.

Oare
Somewhat spoilt by the A345 that carves its way through the centre of the village, this is nevertheless a lovely spot, with some beautiful houses, as well as a pub (the White Hart) offering accommodation and all day food.

Seend Cleeve

If you follow the recommended route then this village will be viewed rather than visited. However, it is adjacent to the main route where the Kennet and Avon Canal passes the Barge Inn and comes within a hair's breadth at Seend Head Mill.

Perhaps not the most memorable village on the way, but one that marks the true central point of the walk and that is the gateway to the Kennet and Avon Canal. Some lovely houses and surprisingly pleasant views can be espied as one passes through the more elevated part of the village if following the alternative route. The Barge Inn, beside the canal, is a popular spot for the consumption of food and liquid refreshment.

Keevil

One of Wiltshire's finest villages, this serene spot is chock-full of gorgeous houses and possesses both a walled manor and a delightful church. However, there is nowhere to pause for refreshments, so be sure to have your own supplies if you want to stay for any length of time.

Steeple Ashton

This most attractive village is dominated by a lovely church and a wonderful main street, where visions of yesteryear will cause one to stop and ponder.

Don't miss the village's superb community shop which, staffed by volunteers, is open long hours, has copious supplies and serves a wide range of snacks, sandwiches and drinks in a small incorporated café.

Perhaps Steeple Ashton's most alluring charms are derived from its combination of architectural and scenic splendour in a quiet and peaceful context, a blend which many better known English villages cannot match.

Bratton

Containing some truly historic and distinct dwellings, this small settlement will not disappoint. That said, the way only clips the village edge, so you will need to leave the way to appreciate its charms in full.

Upton Scudamore

A truly delightful spot, meeting the expectation of those seeking the quintessential English village. The Angel Inn – an upmarket gourmet style pub – and an exquisite church, set in an elevated position, with fabulous views to Cley Hill, give the village lasting appeal. Unsurprisingly, both food and accommodation are available, though perhaps not for those on a tight budget.

Horningsham

Perhaps no village is more picturesque on the entire Way than this picture-postcard one! However, it is not so much the village centre that draws the eye, but rather the setting and wonderfully scenic surroundings. Cottages – spread over quite a large area and sometimes quite isolated from other dwellings – chapels and churches, set against a backdrop of rolling green hills, provide the walker with a rich supply of mouth-watering visual delights. These attractions will at the very least cause you to ponder and may well bring you to a complete halt as you stop in an attempt to comprehend the beauty of your surroundings.

To visit the village centre you will need to depart briefly from the route but this is a small price to pay for the pleasures encountered.

Kingston Deverill

Deliciously rural and nestling at the heart of the Deverill valley, this village appears to occupy an almost forgotten corner of the county. Forgotten that is by all except those inhabitants who ensure that this spot retains its timeless charms. The peace and serenity that radiates from the centre of this small settlement has to be experienced to be believed, with cottages, a church and the infant Wylye providing innumerable reasons for a slowing of the pace and even a non-scheduled stop. However, there are currently no accommodation or refreshment facilities available, but don't let this concern you; Mere is not far away and the lack of commercial activity (that even a village pub can generate), ensures the tranquillity of this village is rarely disturbed.

Mere

This is such a fitting village from which to start or finish a long distance walk! As well as an abundant supply of accommodation and excellent local services, a considerable range of architectural sights compete for your attention.

A centrally placed, very friendly café (the Angel Corner), serves as the ideal spot at which to celebrate your journey's end, contemplate further wanderings or plan a return trip.

Mere, nestled neatly in the vale

Accommodation in brief

The Mid-Wilts Way has not been devised primarily with accommodation needs in mind. However, the route's six stages have been based on both a rough equality of distance and, whenever possible, the practical accessibility of accommodation options. I believe this is the right way round – the route first, practicalities second – however I am also one of those walkers who shares a love of comfortable accommodation at the end of the day. After all, many a fine walking experience is enhanced by the creature comforts enjoyed at the start and finish of the endeavour.

All but one section of the walk ends with at least one accommodation option without the need to leave the route. However, don't always expect a huge choice, sometimes the village featured at a section's end has just one or two hospitality providers.

It goes without saying that the provision of accommodation changes quite regularly, so careful planning is required to avoid disappointment. That said, accommodation options are just as likely to improve as decline. Thus, if the Mid-Wilts Way proves to be popular it may encourage others to provide shelter for weary walkers.

The one stage of the Way without any accommodation options (Tan Hill) is also rather too far from the nearest settlement which possesses them. Thus you will probably need to walk on to the end of the next stage or stake out a different itinerary. Alternative ideas are offered with the route description and under the heading Suggested Itineraries on page 74.

Recommended maps

The most practical maps for the Mid-Wilts Way are probably those from the Landranger series. Sheets 173, 184 and 183 cover the route (in that order, east-to-west), although the walk only clips the north-west corner of 184. Landranger maps are excellent for their trade-off between manageability and detail. However, as field boundaries are not marked, it would be wise to study the relevant OS Explorer maps in conjunction, before setting out, and/or to carry them in your rucksack in case of emergency.

Such is the quality of British OS maps that there is little need for any further discussion at this point, other than to say that the sketch maps provided in this guide book are intended only to provide a general overview of Way's six stages so that all those walking the Way should set out with the relevant set of maps or have them easily to hand.

Waymarking, rights of way and access

Every care has been taken to ensure that, at all times, the route utilises either rights of way or, very occasionally, permissive paths, and, further, that the route enjoys official status, being supported by Wiltshire County Council and included as a waymarked trail (diamond symbol) on both Landranger and Explorer OS maps.

Following the initial planning of the route the invaluable assistance of the senior rights of way technician at Wiltshire County Council was sought, without whose help the Way would probably never have made it into print. Additionally, many other people have provided vitally important support and guidance to ensure that the walk has avoided controversy and has been established with the widest possible consensual backing. That said, no funding has been secured for the Way's waymarking or promotion. Even relevant charitable associations have not taken part in any waymarking or promotion.

What does this mean on the ground? Well, I hope walkers will agree that the route is simple to follow and adequately but discretely waymarked. It is simple to follow because almost all of the route follows well established rights of way, and it is appropriately waymarked because I personally carried out the operation (with guidance and advice from Wiltshire County Council) and continue to maintain it on a regular basis, living only minutes from the central point of the walk. Some stretches are less frequently waymarked than others, but this is for good reason and not due to any lack of waymarking materials. Note, in particular, that there are no waymarks on the Kennet and Avon Canal, save where the route joins and leaves it. This avoids cluttering a busy area where the Way is simple to follow in any case. Similarly, the road sections are not waymarked. In short, for those competent with a map and/or guide book it should be hard to go wrong for long; even if you do take a wrong turn, the added pleasures experienced may well more than compensate for any frustration caused. The author would welcome any feedback about waymarking, etc., which should be addressed to the publisher.

Despite increased access to the countryside as a result of steady legislative progress over the years, perhaps more than ever before it is necessary not to offend landowners when publishing new routes by assuming access rights exist where careful research demonstrates otherwise. Thousands now visit the countryside for relaxation and leisure and take advantage of perhaps the most privileged access to private land anywhere in the world. Routes short and long, official and unofficial, written and deliberately informal, proliferate throughout the UK placing, at times, a considerable strain on sensitive agricultural land. Many farmers have stories to tell of inconsiderate walkers (of course the reverse is sometimes true too) and therefore all responsible walkers, especially those wishing to commit routes to print, must ensure that every effort has been made to follow routes that are *bona fide* beyond question, without obstruction and likely to remain so in future.

The Mid-Wilts Way, based on these principles, is therefore not a controversial route at any point. That said, the author did engage in substantial negotiations to try to secure access over private land where no right of way existed. The results of these negotiations were genuinely mixed but only affect three relatively small areas of the entire route, namely Cley Hill and the Longleat Estate in Stage 5, and the Deverill ridge in Stage 6.

Cley Hill, when approached from the east and north, is a splendid prospect, and a route from this angle would have been both aesthetically pleasing and perhaps more logical than the official one from the east and south which involves an out-and-back section. Additionally, the link between the approaching right of way and National Trust open access land is across uncultivated, unfenced grass which takes less than two minutes to negotiate. However, the landowner had very real concerns about the implications of opening a new route from the north, fearing that many more walkers would wish to pass through (and possibly block lanes on) his land to access the hill. Although I suggested that a non-waymarked route, of low-key status, would have sufficed, he understandably foresaw an equality issue where casual strollers, spotting Mid-Wilts Way walkers leaving and joining the hill from the north, would cry foul if they were forbidden access. Further, as is sadly too often the case, the farmer has also experienced rudeness and aggression from walkers recently that has left him profoundly wary of the implications of extended access opportunities.

Separately, a potentially glorious route through the Longleat Estate was earnestly sought over a period of months, but was repeatedly turned down over concerns about the route potentially setting in stone walking rights through the Estate. Thus access was not the issue, but 'access in print' very much was. This means that the official route has to pass along the roadside for a mile and a half until a bridleway leads off the road to the village of Horningsham. However, this cloud has a definite silver lining, because independent minded walkers are at liberty to close their guide book and make their way, at their own risk, through the Estate, via Heaven's Gate – a magnificent viewpoint – to Horningsham, there to rejoin the waymarked route. (For more information see the section entitled Lane and Road Sections on page 20.)

Ending on a positive note, the third area over which negotiations took place concerned the glorious stretch over the Deverill ridge between Horningsham and Kingston Deverill. While on the ridge beside the fence, the right of way eventually diverts away from the same to ascend Cold Kitchen Hill, heading in a north-easterly direction, over cultivated land, before turning sharp south, past a partridge shoot, to head off the ridge toward Kingston Deverill. In what was a very magnanimous gesture, the landowner agreed to my alternative proposal that the route should follow the fence, continuing on an uncultivated strip-cum-track in an unbroken east-south-east direction to reach a little gate where walkers would rejoin the official right of way, heading south to Kingston Deverill. I would like to stress that this compromise suits all parties admirably and therefore should be carefully and responsibly followed.

Access to the route at both ends, as well as at numerous points on the walk, is excellent. However, where the route passes through fields, you may at times have to contend with farm animals and, during the winter, their effects on the land, e.g., mud baths at gates between fields. The use of country lanes has been deliberately included to minimise such problems where they are likely to be most common but, overall, the route is often gloriously uncomplicated, leaving the walker ample opportunity to appreciate the wonderful surroundings without the need to constantly keep an eye on what concerns lay ahead or underfoot.

Weather on the walk

Wiltshire weather is as benign as almost anywhere else in the UK. Rainfall is moderate (30-40 inches per year), land above 1,000 feet non-existent, and sunshine a regular companion throughout the seasons. Yes, there are times when rain sweeps over the hills and strong winds blow, and occasionally the highest tops are temporarily dusted with the white stuff, but it's all very tame compared with Britain's upland areas, and the exception – severe weather – just serves to prove the rule. Few days in the year will produce weather to prevent you from walking the Way.

However, conditions underfoot can be a different matter. The higher ground is rarely a problem but some of the lowland paths can become very boggy. Road and lane sections cut out some of these problems but, if undertaking this route in winter – a good time in so many other respects – conditions underfoot may be trying. Still, if you find yourself sat on your rear end without intention, at least you will have an extra story to tell and a guide book writer to blame.

Equipment required

Another benefit of lowland walking is that the kinder climate is a lot less exacting, and thus a fortune need not be spent on suitable clothing. Heavy boots and top-of-the-range Gortex items are unnecessary and for most of the year a few light layers will probably suffice.

That said, common sense dictates that certain items should be included on your list of essentials. A waterproof coat should be carried in all but the most settled summer weather and a good pair of light-weight boots, with adequate ankle support, will prove considerably more suitable than any other form of footwear. Clothes made from synthetic, rather than natural fibres such as cotton, will be far more comfortable in all seasons, helping the body remain sweat-free. Additionally, a warm hat and gloves will help the body to retain essential heat during the colder months when winds can be chilly on the tops of the Downs. During the summer, a cap may also help shield you from the effects of strong sunshine.

A brooding storm hovering over the Downs, viewed to superb effect from Knapp Hill

Other than this, much is down to personal preference and, should you find yourself inadequately clad, you are unlikely to be in a life-threatening situation as a result. (Ironically, when walking the route on a January day, the winds were especially strong and at one particular point combined with a violent downpour to mock my rather relaxed approach to clothing in particular. However, once the storm abated, sweeping blue skies returned and stayed my companion, resolutely, for the remainder of the day). One should, of course, approach the choice of clothing with care, and getting it right will add considerably to the quality of your experience, but the margin for error is far greater, and the necessary budget much smaller than either will ever be for those planning a mountain or upland expedition.

Lane and road sections on the Mid-Wilts Way

Road walking in the countryside has largely come to be regarded as a contradiction in terms. This is understandable as rural walks are embarked upon, in part at least, to escape the pace and noise of life, as typified on our modern, open roads. Further, glancing at the Mid-Wilts Way route profile, one might draw the conclusion that a little too much of it makes use of lanes and roads, even when alternatives appear to be available. Bearing these thoughts in mind I believe it is necessary to provide a brief explanation concerning the road and some lane sections included and the rationale behind their inclusion.

If following the A361 (alternative route, Stage 3) from Seend Cleeve to the turning for Keevil, considerable care is needed to negotiate this short stretch safely; however, it may be bypassed fully by following the main route to Seend Head Mill. Then, on the approach to Keevil, the initial country road leaving the A361 is quiet and the lane off of it quieter still. Thus, although this stretch could largely be covered across open countryside, the lanes provide a blend of pleasant surroundings and the opportunity for good progress. When one bears in mind the amount of open country crossed throughout the entire walk, and the all year round appeal of the walk, this is perhaps no bad thing, balancing peace, scenic splendour and practical progress in one.

The road joined just outside of Dunge and followed to Bratton (Stage 4) is more controversial. Thus, as well as an explanation in the text itself, further justification at this point is provided. When I first tried out this stretch I followed the White Horse Trail. Admittedly it was during winter, but it was nevertheless a real slog. Incredibly boggy field entrances/exits represented an exercise in staying upright, whilst boots were nearly submerged in the mud. Taking a wrong turn I arrived at the railway line with no way of crossing it in prospect. Retracing my steps I was then confronted with a sign warning 'Bull in the Field', which seemed to sum up this venture, so I abandoned this rather slow and fruitless attempt and decided to try the road instead.

Lane walking takes on a whole new meaning on the Mid-Wilts Way

This was an altogether more positive experience. The road in question is wide and has generous verges, enabling walkers to keep well out of the way of passing cars. Further, fast, straightforward progress is accompanied by open, sweeping views, in which the Edington and Westbury Downs are delightfully prominent. Anyone walking the way can, of course, forsake it when joining the road and follow the White Horse Trail instead. During the summer this may well be a pleasant alternative. The choice is all yours, but do of course take care if you follow the official route.

The very short stretch besides the A36 (Stage 5) is an unfortunate necessity but is perfectly safe and need not last for more than a few minutes. Additionally, this stretch only serves to prove just how tranquil, peaceful and sublimely rural the vast majority of the walk is.

Finally, some readers may be disappointed at the inclusion of the road section between Cley Hill and Horningsham. A route through the glorious Longleat Estate would have been a great alternative, not just because it avoids the road, but because of its scenic splendour and unique character, adding yet another dimension to the Way. However, Estate managers wanted to preserve existing access arrangements which, though generous, do not extend to permission for routes to be committed to print. This may appear ironic, as many walkers do of course walk through the Estate. However, don't be downcast because, if you close your guide book and make your own way through the Estate, at your own risk, you will not have committed any offence.

Should you choose to stick with the official route, be very careful as you pass along the brief stretch of the A362, which is narrow in places. After the roundabout, the unclassified road to Horningsham is wide and straight for most of its course and provides pleasant wooded surroundings but, shortly before you leave it, there is a brief section of slight bends that need to be passed with care. Try to ensure you are wearing bright colours and avoid walking this stretch in twilight or on a dull winter's day. Had this one and a half mile section not been included the walk would have to have been terminated at Cley Hill, an unacceptable price to pay when considering the delights in store between Horningsham and Mere, one of the finest Stages of the entire walk.

For your peace of mind, road walking accounts for less than

ten per cent of the entire Mid-Wilts Way. Lanes are not included in this calculation because, as discussed above, they have been deliberately incorporated and do not equate, in any way, to walking along the roadside.

Great views and wide verges on the Dunge to Bratton road

Using the Guide

I trust you will find this guide useful for more than one purpose. First, the intention is to combine the background and practical information about the route with a description of some of the Way's more alluring features, to stimulate interest and provide inspiration. Then, preceded by an individual section summary – in short an overview of the route, along with highlights to be anticipated and experienced – a section-by-section route description is included in an attempt to ensure that walkers can complete the walk in confidence. Further, the description of the route includes additional information on points of interest relevant to the Stage being described. The purpose of these inserts is to provide a little background information in an attractive manner, so that your step may be quickened at the thought of what's to come in the Stage ahead and your knowledge of the Way's context and history broadened just a little.

The six Stages are not intended to equate to day long expeditions but rather to divide the walk into manageable sections that can be suitably planned. In fact, many walkers will comfortably walk two Stages in a day and, where accommodation is not available without leaving the Way or is in short supply, carrying on to the end of the next Stage may prove a more practical option.

It is no secret, of course, that many walkers choose to walk long distance paths in several broken stretches. The six Stages lend themselves well to such an approach. Providing you are fit and ambitious all six Stages should be manageable in a long day, on an out-and-back basis, during spring, summer and early autumn seasons. For more information on this type of itinerary see page 76.

A genuine attempt has been made to describe the route in an interesting and engaging manner. Otherwise, there is a danger that the main body of any walking guide book becomes too matter of fact, lacking essential encouragement.

As already mentioned, the maps in this book are provided as a visual overview of the route and thus should not be used for navigation purposes. Further, despite the route descriptions, all walkers are advised to carry either the relevant Landranger or Explorer maps with them, and to have the map set for each stage of the walk. A small error on the ground could cause problems or be a source of irritation to landowners, so do try to bear this in mind at all times.

Deciding in which direction to describe the route was hugely difficult because both options have almost equal merit. In fact, for a long time I fully intended to describe the route in both directions, as is now often the practice with long distance walking guide books. However, I did eventually decide that the westward direction had the edge. That said, nothing can beat the approach to the final section of the Pewsey Downs from the East, most especially where the Downs sharply terminate above Wootton Rivers and a vast swathe of Wiltshire and Berkshire.

By way of personal recommendation I would suggest you walk the route in both directions, either as day-long, out-and-back Stages or, better still, as two separate, continuous, multi-day walks. If you think the guide can be improved in any way, please pass on your comments to the publisher.

Getting to/from the walk

Accessing either end of the walk is easiest for those of you with either your own vehicle (if you are walking the stages on an out-and-back basis) or a kind friend who can deposit you in Wootton Rivers and collect you again in Mere. However, there are some public transport options if you cannot reach the Way by car.

Pewsey is fortunate to have a mainline station and from there it is relatively easy to reach the village of Oare by bus; ideal for those pursuing a four-day itinerary that commences with a quite short, circular first day (see Suggested Itineraries, page 74). At the other end of the Way, Mere is not far from Gillingham which also has a train station.

Various other points on the Mid-Wilts Way can be accessed by public transport but, as services tend to vary, both on a seasonal and longer term basis, I would recommend you contact the relevant TIC (see page 73) to seek out current information. For train times, you could of course check the National Rail Enquiries website, which is surprisingly user friendly and provides up to date details.

The Country Code

The precious access we enjoy to our countryside and upland areas is truly remarkable and thus everyone has a duty to follow the country code in earnest. Just in case you need reminding, the code is given overleaf:

- Guard against all risk of fire
- Fasten all gates
- Keep dogs under control
- Keep to public paths across farmland, and avoid taking short cuts which cause erosion
- Use gates and stiles to cross fences, hedges and walls
- Leave livestock, crops and machinery alone
- Take your litter home
- Help to keep all water clean
- Protect wildlife, plants and tress
- Take special care on country roads
- Make no unnecessary noise.

On a personal note I would also add that this walk is far from ideal for dogs for much of the way, because of the livestock regularly encountered. Further, try to avoid walking the route in large groups, and enjoy it instead as a solitary walk or one to be enjoyed as a couple or with a small group of friends/family.

The Route:

Wootton Rivers to Mere

Key to Maps:
- - - - Main Route
——— Road, lane or track

Key to text:
Paragraphs describing the route are in normal type; visible features or changes of direction are highlighted in **bold**; those not concerned with giving directions are in *italics*.
Right and left are abbreviated as R and L. The Mid-Wilts Way is referred to as MWW throughout.

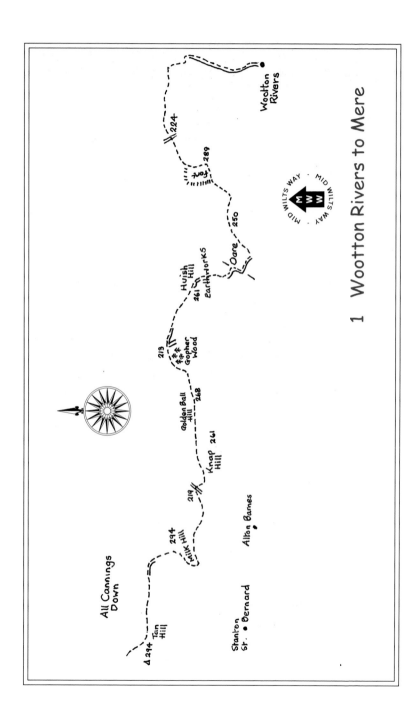

1 Wootton Rivers to Mere

Stage 1: Wootton Rivers to Tan Hill

Distance:	11m, 17km
Maps:	Landranger 173, Explorer 157
Accommodation:	Wootton Rivers, Oare, Horton off-route
Food and Drink:	Wootton Rivers, Oare

The walk begins in the delightful village of Wootton Rivers on the bridge over the Kennet and Avon Canal, which will be joined later on the way. Thatched cottages dominate the scene, vying for your attention this way and that, as you stride along the quiet village street. Soon you will leave the village on a bridleway, passing through a boulevard of trees.

Paths with pleasant views lead to Martinsell Hill and the start of the glorious Pewsey Downs. At their eastern end the Downs reach an abrupt and steep climax providing, unsurprisingly, mouth-watering views. These extend, when clear conditions prevail, from the Marlborough Downs in the north, to Savernake Forest, Inkpen Hill and all the way to the familiar chimney beneath Westbury White Horse way in the West.

Several miles of fabulous downland with steep southern escarpments accompany your every step, until the Downs merge into a plateau west of Tan Hill - the equal highest summit in Wiltshire.

Here Stage 1 ends, but finding accommodation will involve a considerable detour south and west to the small village of Horton. This may be a possible option for those with time aplenty and a reluctance to leave this lovely part of the county but practicalities may require most walkers to include Stages 1 & 2 in their Day 1 plans. A further option could be to start the walk with a short half-day, pausing for accommodation in the village of Oare, which is directly en route, or you could decide to make Day 1 a circular affair, starting and ending in Oare, using quiet lanes between Wootton Rivers and Martinsell Hill to avoid retracing your steps entirely, before pushing on to Devizes on Day 2.

The authentic starting point is at the southern end of the village, on the bridge over the **Kennet and Avon Canal** (see above) which, some 20 miles later, will be joined and followed to the half-way point of the Way. As you walk through the village delightful dwellings (many of them thatched) compete for your attention to the left and right. In a few moments you will pass the **Royal Oak**, which offers food and accommodation.

Towards the edge of the village, with a **thatched house** straight ahead, a **fork** of sorts is reached. Take the **L** option, leaving the road to join a track. Already the surroundings are delightfully rural, and to your left the dramatic eastern terminus of the Pewsey Downs can be seen.

Passing shortly through a boulevard of trees, the route starts to climb slowly; at the top of this **gentle slope**, turn **L** keeping to the field edge, and enjoy lovely views to the south, which feature the hills that form the backdrop to the Vale of Pewsey.

When you shortly reach a **fence** turn **R** and follow an obvious line of trees. The field path soon brings you to **Mud Lane** (for much of the year very aptly, if even somewhat generously, named), where you need to turn **L**. Follow the lane all the way to the **road**. After crossing the road pass through a **small car park**, conveniently placed for access to the Pewsey Downs, which are now straight ahead of you.

The stretch you will now be passing over has been designated as open access land, so a degree of freedom can be enjoyed as you climb the escarpment to access the tops of the Downs. Soon emerging on the crest, turn naturally **L** keeping the boundary **fence** to your **R**.

A huge swathe of Wiltshire and Berkshire is laid out before you, providing a scene of rural tranquillity that seems so improbable in today's world, but your eyes will not be deceiving you: this is southern England at its best!

Continuing along the crest you come to a **small gate** followed immediately by a **bench** on the **L**. At this point you are in fact taking a right-angled turn to follow the Downs westwards, with miles of high level walking ahead of you.

Keeping the **fence** to your **L** pass through a small wooded area and then walk besides the fence again in a more open setting. Shortly you will spy a **gate**, immediately after which you need to **cross the fence** via a lowered wooden section, suitable for safe human passage and a quite common feature in these parts. Then, ignoring a grassy downhill track, stay high on open access land, keeping the **fence** to your **R**.

Very soon a superb view (especially west but east and all around too) will once again cause you to gaze and wonder. The beauty and drama of this spot cannot adequately be put into words, but central to its qualities is the profile of the Downs and their steep southern slopes, as well as an almost neverending valley running out beyond the chimney beneath Westbury White Horse, some 20 miles away as the crow flies. Looking behind you, Inkpen Hill adds additional poignancy. Thus you may find yourself turning 360 degrees, a number of times, to take it all in. This indeed marks one of the finest stretches of the entire walk!

Follow the crest of the Downs along what becomes an increasingly narrow and airy ridge to pass ancient burial grounds, and then a prominent **trig point**. Now the ridge plunges spectacularly into a **field** where you curve **L** to reach a **stile** in the corner. Once over the stile keep the field edge to your immediate **L** at first and then head straight across to a **gate** leading onto a **lane**. Turn **R** and follow this pretty lane to the main road, the A345. **Cross** the road and pass the **White Hart** pub, turning **L** immediately after into a lane signed to **Huish**. After a row of cottages turn **R** and head once again up onto the Downs. It is a steep but exhilarating climb, with a **bench** near the top to spur you on.

After enjoying more gorgeous views, head a little further **uphill** and then turn **L** (west) and shortly pass through a **gate** (open access land and much more simple to follow than the rather convoluted right of way). Now simply keep the **fence** to your **R**, steep scarp slopes to your **L** and enjoy this superb, belvedere stretch.

As you descend towards **Gopher Wood** you will notice the unmistakable earthwork to the **R** (the evidence of ancient human activity is a constant feature of this walk). When you reach a **cross-track** on the edge of the woods, cross it and head gently

uphill, with the earthwork and wood as close companions. At the **next gate** take a **diagonal L**. Once again you are approaching the tops of the Downs and shortly you will be gazing out over the Vale of Pewsey, drinking in magnificent views with almost every step. Once you have reached the scarp slopes head west.

Passing through occasional gates and riding high on the Downs, continue to **Knapp Hill**. You may be tempted to skirt this remarkable hill to the **R**, but that would be a mistake as it not only provides more glorious views but is also a wonderful vantage point from which to study the character of the dramatic southern slopes of the Downs, especially to the east.

When you have drunk your fill of this summit panorama, drop off the hill westwards to a **small car park** beside the road. **Cross** the road and walk along the verge for a few metres. Then cross a **stile** on your **R** and head towards the summit of **Walker's Hill**.

Summit panoramas are now familiar but no less appealing, not least because each individual summit offers its own unique vantage point. The particular appeal of this hill is that it affords outstanding views of the Downs in both directions, due largely to the fact that it protrudes southwards.

Head west over the Downs past **Alton Barnes White Horse** – a scruffy, dull and faded affair which nevertheless can be seen from miles around – and follow the **scarp edge** as it almost doubles back on itself in the vicinity of **Milk Hill**. After a superbly aesthetic U-shaped curve, take a **R** heading north, through a **weighted gate**. Heading briefly over what is, in effect, the outer fringes of the Milk Hill plateau, reach another **weighted gate** to join immediately after, the Wansdyke path – your elevated companion for several miles to come.

Following the **Wansdyke** westward (to the **L** as you join it), **Tan**

Hill is reached (or rather passed) almost as an afterthought, the way not passing over the summit of what is, like Milk Hill before it, a plateau rather than a pointy perch.

The Pewsey Downs

The Pewsey Downs form a nature reserve supporting a rich diversity of plant and bird life. This is in large part due to their uncultivated yet close-cropped character, where the absence of agricultural management and the activity of grazing sheep have combined to splendid effect. But this is only part of the picture! The Downs are simultaneously a long continuous ridge with a steep-sided southern scarp edge and a series of hills with real individual character. Further, nowhere in Wiltshire are downland views so extensive, providing a panorama that incorporates miles of Wiltshire countryside, as well as, at times, almost the entire shapely ridge. Perhaps nowhere is this experienced to greater effect than where the ridge drops from the east into Oare. Here it first narrows on both sides before plunging steeply into quiet fields at the edge of the village.

Opposite above: The Pewsey Downs are a stirring sight, and as they occupy the highest ground in the county, views from their various summits are unrivalled

Opposite below: Where the Downs fall abruptly to the East of Oare, they take on a mini-upland form

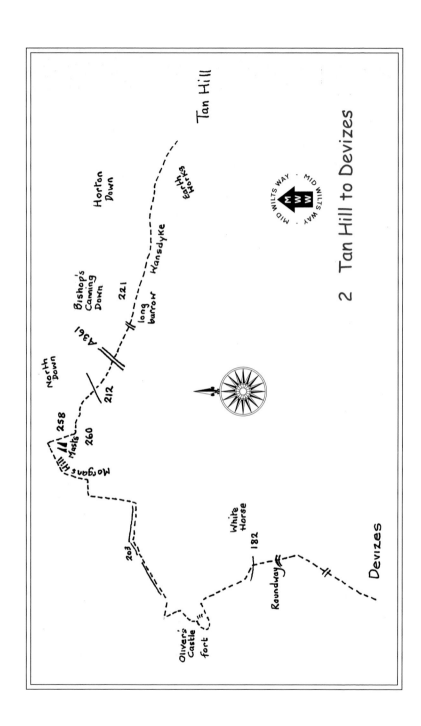

Tan Hill

Horton Down

Earth Works

Mansdyke

long barrow

221

Bishop's Canning Down

A361

212

North Down

258

Masts

260

Morgans Hill

203

Oliver's Castle fort

White Horse

182

Roundway

Devizes

MID WILTS WAY · MID WILTS WAY ·

2 Tan Hill to Devizes

Stage 2: Tan Hill to Devizes

Distance:	9.25m, 14.25km
Maps:	Landranger 173, Explorer 157, 156
Accommodation:	Calstone Wellington, Devizes
Food and Drink:	Heddington, Devizes

This stage offers very contrasting features with those experienced so far. A historical theme now dominates as you traverse what is, in effect, a plateau with long distance views. However, it is the extraordinary man-made structure – known as Wansdyke – that provides the strong historical flavour. But that is not all it provides for the dyke, though rising only a metre or two above the surrounding ground, provides a ridge top perspective without which the walk would be a lesser experience. Peace and quiet are in plentiful supply, except where the way crosses the A361. Beyond this point serenity returns and Morgan's Hill draws closer, promising more far-reaching views as far as the horizon.

Roundway Hill soon follows, providing yet more long-range vistas, most notably to the south-west and the Westbury Downs, before the way descends gracefully into the town of Devizes, the only settlement of any size on the entire route.

Stages 1&2, if combined, make for quite a long day, but one that is not unduly arduous. Further, you will be rewarded with all manner of precious memories to mull over.

A glance at the map could lead you to think that the walk along the Wansdyke might be one of the less interesting stages of the MWW. However nothing could be further from the truth. If, like me, you are privileged to walk this stretch on a bright, clear day, you may well find yourself blown away (figuratively speaking) by the experience and surroundings. The dyke provides not just an extraordinary lesson in British historical field archaeology, but an amazing ridge-like perch, from which to view the vast landscapes all around and especially to the north, where the Cherhill Monument is predominant.

Follow the obvious line along the **Wansdyke** all the way to the **A361**, which is reached immediately after passing between a farmhouse and outbuildings.

Cross the road taking a few steps to the **L** and continue along the dyke. Soon you arrive at a **gate** and **cross track**. Head across the track slightly to the **R**, passing through the trees to reach another **gate**, before rejoining the dyke. Once again follow the dyke, briefly no longer occupying the highest ground, which is now just to the L. The **Cherhill Monument** is now close at hand, the surrounding land looking impressively wild and uncultivated.

Soon you will reach the **twin masts** signalling your imminent arrival at **Morgan's Hill**, but just before the masts branch **R** and head in the direction of the field **fence**. Keeping close to this fence, head for a **stile** in the right-hand corner of this open area, which comes into view as you begin to loose height. Cross it and turn **L** to Morgan's Hill, open access land.

This incredibly poignant spot – the most northerly point on the MWW – provides more vast and lovely views, well beyond Calne, the town at the foot of the hill, towards a horizon that seems so far distant. Morgan's Hill, like many other sections of the MWW, is a nature reserve enjoying both protection and excellent access rights.

After a delightful stretch close to the top of the hill, you will reach a **gate** on your **L** adjacent to the **North Wilts Golf Club**. Pass through the **gate** and turn **L**, then **R** following a path with a **fence** on your L. Following further signs, pick your way across

The Wansdyke – an extraordinary path oozing historical significance and offering lofty, far reaching views

As well as a nature reserve, Morgan's Hill is a splendid viewpoint looking north beyond Calne

the golf course to reach the road in just a few minutes. Cross the road, passing to the L of the **Club House** on a clear track. When the track reaches a crossroads turn **R** into a lane. Follow the lane for some distance, passing some farm buildings, and then when it **forks** take the **L** option, staying high. At the next **fork** branch **R** (straight on in literal terms). Just as the lane is about to descend turn **L** onto a **fenced path**, with views of **Roundway Hill** now straight ahead, and the hill itself only moments away. Soon take a **R** through a **gate** onto Roundway Hill.

Yet another nature reserve and rather like an upland outlier of sorts, this prominent hill, unsurprisingly, provides more sumptuous views, though perhaps not quite as extensive as those enjoyed from Morgan's Hill. However, the hill's own character is more than ample compensation for any views it obscures.

Walk along the crest of the hill, eventually arcing round to the L after completing a U-shaped stroll. Soon you will come to a **fence** (the lovely westward views now behind you and wooded slopes to your R) which you follow to a gate. Here turn **R** then **L** then **R** again, to head along a part-surfaced and wide track, in a southerly direction.

Continue on this track, noting where it starts to bear L, becoming a road simultaneously. The route now begins to descend, offering pleasant views east towards the Pewsey Downs and south, generally in the direction of Devizes. Soon you will reach a large **double gate** on your R. Pass through the gate and head downhill to another road, crossing a **stile** on the way. On reaching the **road** turn **L** and just **after the bend** take a **R**, heading across the fields southwards, to pass via a cross track into another field/wide open area. Continue on an **obvious path** heading broadly south-west. This path is increasingly surfaced underfoot, making for good progress.

When you shortly reach a road, cross it and continue on what is now **Quaker's Walk path** (marked on Explorer maps). This lane becomes increasingly attractive, especially when lined by trees on either side. Follow it until you reach the **Kennet & Avon Canal** close to the centre of **Devizes**.

Stage 2 ends in a far more obvious and logical manner than Stage 1 and may well come as a relief to weary walkers looking for accommodation and home-style comforts. Make the most of it though, as this is the only town through which the MWW passes.

The Wansdyke

Thought probably to have been constructed in the 5th or 6th century by Britons to deter Saxon invaders, this dyke is a truly remarkable feature of the MWW. The bank and ditch earthwork is actually fifty miles in length, linking Inkpen in the east with the Bristol Channel in the west! However, as well as boggling the mind when attempting to comprehend the achievements of its constructors, it also serves as a superb belvedere from which to absorb the surrounding, intensely rural, landscape. Thus on this dyke, historic poignancy and lofty perch combine, to provide a glorious stretch of walking that would undoubtedly be inferior without it.

Roundway Hill

Roundway Hill looks like it has been plucked straight from the Brecon Beacons, downsized and placed precisely, in an area of lovely Wiltshire countryside. Prominent from miles around, it is, unsurprisingly, a magnificent vantage point, offering views that extend from the Westbury Downs to the south-west, across rural lowlands, to Chittoe to the north-west. However, besides taking in and enjoying the sumptuous views, a brief study of the hill's unique character is well worthwhile too. More individualistic than much of Wiltshire's downland, its finger-like, uncultivated spurs draw the eye and invite exploration.

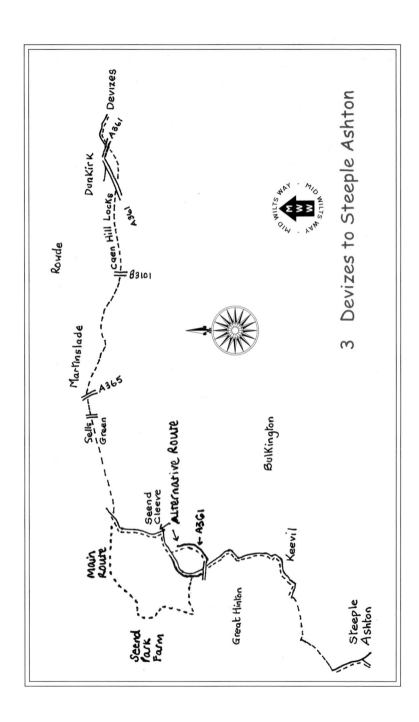

Devizes

A361

DunKirk

Caen Hill Locks

A361

B3101

Rowde

Martinslade

A365

Sells
Green

Seend
Cleeve

Alternative Route

← A361

Bulkington

Main
Route

Keevil

Seend
Park
Farm

Great Hinton

Steeple
Ashton

MID WILTS WAY · MID WILTS WAY · MID WILTS WAY

3   Devizes to Steeple Ashton

Stage 3: Devizes to Steeple Ashton

Distance:	9m, 14km
Maps:	Landranger 173, Explorer 156,143
Accommodation:	Steeple Ashton
Food and Drink:	Seend Cleeve, Steeple Ashton

The way leaves Devizes via the Kennet & Avon Canal (K&A), a hugely popular tourist trail, both on the water and by the towpath. In a short while the impressive spectacle of Caen Hill Locks is passed where, on a hill of some note, no less than 16 continuous locks grab one's attention.

Once the Canal arrives at the village of Seend Cleeve, the former is left behind, and after some pleasant lane walking the village of Keevil is reached. This is a gorgeous little settlement deep in rural Wiltshire, despite its excellent access to the A361. The route leaves the village via its delightful church and graveyard, and soon the church of Steeple Ashton can be seen across the fields, its tower reaching above the trees. These two villages – Keevil and Steeple Ashton – are as fine as any on the entire walk and will reward more detailed exploration.

Joining the **K&A Canal** at this point is a delight, not just because some rapid progress can be made if so desired, but because the extraordinary spectacle of **Caen Hill locks** will soon serve as an interesting accompaniment. After passing a few locks from the centre of Devizes westwards, the towpath reaches the summit of Caen Hill, where a line of locks flow downhill, in a neat and orderly fashion. A **K&A Information Centre** and **tea shop** can easily be accessed at the top of Caen Hill, via a bridge over the canal. Then as you continue beyond the foot of the hill a stretch of gentle canal walking provides a pleasant contrast with all that has gone before and is to come.

Continue on the **towpath** to **Seend Park Farm**, leaving the Canal via a **swing bridge**, passing besides the farm and crossing a stream to reach a **lane T-junction**. Continue along this lane which soon becomes straight and open as it heads towards the **A361**. Just as you reach this main road, a **L** turn is taken to follow a quiet **bridleway**, that becomes increasingly unkempt as it heads towards **Seend Head Mill**. The author and others work hard to keep the latter stretch of the path in passable condition, but don't be surprised if you encounter large stinging nettles and a plethora of other vegetation. When you emerge from the trees, spy the **stile** leading into a **field** and then follow the river to a **gate**, through which you turn **R**. Now follow the lane to arrive in moments at a **T-junction** with the **A361**.

Keevil: a delightfully peaceful and pretty village on the MWW

Take a **L** here, crossing the **road** and then turn almost immediately **R**, into a quiet country **lane** signposted to

Bulkington and Keevil.

Alternative Option

If you want to pass through the village of Seend Cleeve and/or pause overnight, you can follow the alternative route described here instead.

When you reach the **Barge Inn** on the K&A Canal, leave the latter and head gently uphill into the village. When almost at the T-junction on the **A361** take a **R** into **Row Lane** and enjoy lovely views west over a continuously rural landscape. The cottages and larger dwellings serve as pleasant viewing as you pass along this lane. About half-way between the Row Lane turning and Seend Head Mill (checking the OS map at this point will help considerably) spy a concealed **stile**, with waymark, on your L, which leads between dwellings onto a track/private drive. Follow this to shortly reach the **A361**. Now follow with diligence and care the A361 to the **Keevil** and **Bulkington turning** to rejoin the main route.

After a few minutes turn **R** onto an unsigned lane. If the hedge is not too high and especially if it is winter time, pleasant views can be enjoyed as you stroll along it. At a **T-junction** on the edge of Keevil take a **R** (straight on in literal terms) and follow the lane as it curves round to the R to enter this serene village. If conditions are suitable, look out for gliders climbing into the sky, in an effortless, silent sweep (Keevil has its own small airfield).

Head into the village and pass two turnings on the L to continue with a high wall to your R. Shortly turn **L** into **Church Lane** admiring the fine buildings hereabouts as you do so. The **church** is now straight ahead of you and looks a glorious sight.

Pass through the **graveyard** and to the R of the church, heading over the grass to a **kissing gate**. After the gate spy a little **bridge** ahead of you. Cross this and take a **diagonal L** to reach another **kissing gate**. Now turn **R** and keep to the field edge. Pass through **two more kissing gates** and still keeping close to the field edge admire Steeple Ashton's sixteenth century church, now prominent and ahead of you.

Soon you will join a fenced, grassy **track** immediately after a **gate**. Then follows a slightly confusing moment. Straight ahead you will see an unmistakeable gap in the hedge, through which the route turns L. However on your **R**, just before the gap, is a signed path, followed by a **L** turn leading to a gate and stile, which leads to the gap in the hedge! Assuming you have followed the waymarked path, keep to the field edge and with Steeple Ashton's **church** now straight ahead of you, head down to a little **bridge** in the corner of the field. Cross the bridge and head straight across to a gate. After the **gate**, take a **diagonal R**

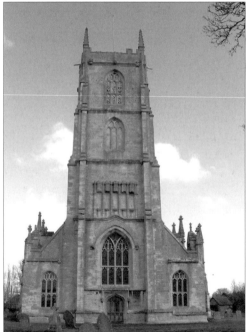

towards the church. Now cross a **stile** and then a **gate** and head straight on. Follow a wide, grassy, fenced **path**, branching **L** to pass through a concealed **kissing gate**, leading into the **churchyard**.

Steeple Ashton's most prominent landmark. More than 500 years old, this church has timeless appeal

It is impossible not to admire the architecture of this splendid, sixteenth century church, which you can now view to splendid effect as you pass through the churchyard.

When you have drunk your fill of this real gem, pass through a **kissing gate** on the **R**, then turn **L**, passing through yet another **kissing gate** to turn **R**. Head along a narrow, brief **path** to, you've guessed it, another **kissing gate**, where you turn **L** to shortly join the main road through the village. When you reach it turn **L**, taking in your extremely pleasant surroundings with every step.

Walk through the village passing the **Longs Arms**, an attractive looking pub that also offers B&B accommodation, and shortly turn **R** into **Acreshort Lane**. Here then Stage 3 comes to an end and Stage 4 begins, and what better way to mark the fact than by pausing to visit the community shop and café. Staffed by volunteers from the village, this shop has an atmosphere of goodwill as well as plentiful supplies and lovely home-made cakes, the ideal accompaniment to a range of hot and cold drinks also provided. To reach the shop, walk past the turning into Acreshort Lane and locate it almost immediately on the R.

The Kennet and Avon (K&A) Canal

This historic, man-made waterway was constructed in the early 1800s to close the gap between the rivers Kennet and Avon. At 57 miles apart, this was no mean feat, the achievements of its engineers being nowhere more apparent than when approaching the town of Devizes from the west. Within a distance of approximately two miles, 29 locks were constructed to make possible the assent of Caen Hill. The hill itself boasts 16 of these locks and is an impressive sight.

The MWW joins the K&A Canal at Devizes, taking in all 29 locks and a further stretch of the towpath, before finally returning to open countryside just beyond the village of Seend Cleeve.

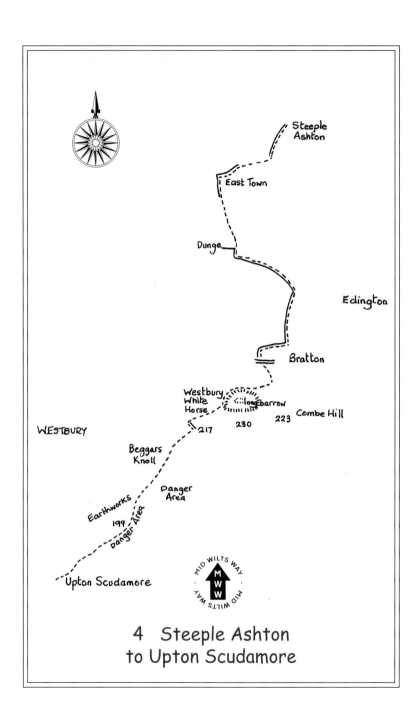

Steeple Ashton

East Town

Dunge

Edington

Bratton

Westbury White Horse

Loosebarrow

Combe Hill

WESTBURY

217

230

223

Beggars Knoll

Danger Area

Earthworks

199

Danger Area

Upton Scudamore

MID WILTS WAY
MID WILTS WAY
M W W

4 Steeple Ashton
to Upton Scudamore

Stage 4: Steeple Ashton to Upton Scudamore

Distance:	9m, 14km
Maps:	Landranger 173,184, 183, Explorer 143
Accommodation:	Upton Scudamore
Food and Drink:	Bratton, Upton Scudamore

Gentle country walking, with lovely views of Wiltshire's extensive downland all around, follows the departure from Steeple Ashton, before you reach the West Ashton to Bratton road. Following this road to Bratton itself, the views ahead and to the right are perhaps as fine as any from the roadside, in the county. The approach ensures that the Westbury Downs seem remarkably extensive and dramatic, in particular the uncultivated area around the White Horse (itself hidden from sight from this angle) is especially impressive, appearing in form like a mini upland expanse.

Ascending the Downs then provides a sense of real achievement, especially as some distance away Steeple Ashton can be seen nestling in the Vale. On a clear day the Pewsey Downs also stand out very clearly, bringing back treasured memories of earlier exploits.

Pressing on, a pleasant ridge-top walk leads to a lovely view of Upton Scudamore and Cley Hill before the route drops down into the village to complete another satisfying stage.

Acreshort Lane is surfaced but is a quiet, serene stretch, far from the madding crowd. The Westbury and Edington Downs are now ahead of you and look increasingly a splendid prospect.

When the road surface ends turn **R** onto a **bridleway**, passing a **bench**. This pleasant, grassy track descends to a **T-junction** of sorts where you turn **R** and then immediately **L**, heading straight on, now gently uphill. Despite hedges on both sides, exquisite views can often be enjoyed all around.

Steeple Ashton: There's nowhere quite like it on the MWW

Follow the track to **East Town**, a tiny hamlet that is as sleepy and peaceful as any settlement on the MWW. When you reach the hamlet turn **L**, keeping farm buildings to your **L** also. The little lane soon becomes a track as you very quickly return to the open countryside.

Now you can enjoy some of the best views from a lowland position on the whole walk. The Pewsey Downs, clearly visible to the East, look like a distant mountain ridge and even the Alton Barnes white horse – that scruffy, grey affair – can be clearly seen!

When the track ends, head straight on and slightly R, keeping close to the **hedge**, which is the field's edge. Increasingly, your eye will be drawn to the Westbury Downs, now looming large ahead.

When the **hedge** turns at a **right-angle**, forsake it and continue straight across to a **gate**, leading on to the West Ashton to Edington road. Turn **L** and follow the road. (You may find, during spring time in particular, that its easier to follow the hedge after all, because the field is somewhat unkempt and features long grass and sometimes oil seed rape.)

You may well be tempted to ask why this road section has been included when nearby the White Horse Trail heads through fields to reach the village of Bratton. The justification for its inclusion is as follows: the road, though at rush hour quite busy, is a minor one, and is wide with generous verges. Further, it is open and offers some of the best roadside views anywhere in the county, featuring the Edington Downs (straight ahead) and the Westbury Downs to the R (south). Finally, the countryside alternative is prone to a number of boggy sections during the colder months and is, at times, heavy and slow going. Thus, all in all I would argue the road choice is a good one. Of course, any walker can forsake it and follow the White Horse Trail to Bratton instead, but that is a choice you can perhaps leave until the day in question.

When you reach a **crossroads** turn **R**, the road is signposted for Bratton and in a short while you cross over the Westbury to Paddington **railway line** via a **bridge**, which precedes the village of Bratton by just a few minutes.

As you enter the village, note the remarkable, thatched **Court House**, now a private dwelling and a real sight to behold. Just after the house turn **R** into Lower Westbury road – a lane leading away from the village. After a few minutes turn **L** into another lane and head uphill to meet and **cross** the B3098.

The Westbury Downs (more appropriately from this angle perhaps, the 'Westbury Uplands') make for a very exciting prospect. Upland connoisseurs will now be licking their lips as they admire the sharp profile of the Downs to their immediate R. When approached from this angle, with the memories of all that has gone before, this is one of the finest ascents of the MWW.

When the sturdy **fence** ends, bear naturally **R**.

But do not do so before taking one last look at the delightful panorama. In particular, if clear conditions prevail, the Pewsey Downs, Roundway Hill and especially, a side on view of the Edington Downs, are a stirring prospect. As a point of fact, it was this very view that, combined with close examination of relevant OS maps, was the inspiration for the MWW.

Continue your ascent and cross a **stile**.

The views to the north out over central Wiltshire are now sublime. Steeple Ashton's church is remarkably prominent, and studying it makes for a poignant moment, as you remember the beautiful village in which it is situated, and the lovely walk that links the village with the Downs which are now underfoot.

In a few moments you will emerge on the very **crest** of the Downs. Follow the crest to the **White Horse**, trying not to trip as the panorama provides a constant distraction.

When you actually reach the White Horse, another remarkable view opens out westwards along the Downs steep northern face. Further, the crest to valley differentials, as you stand atop the horse are impressive, creating a real impression of height

Westbury White Horse

One of Wiltshire's best known landmarks and visible from all over the central regions of the county, Westbury White Horse draws sedentary tourists, casual strollers, paragliders and a host of others to its lofty perch. Wiltshire sports many white horses - there's even a trail named after them - but the steep-slopes and huge panorama at Westbury's are the biggest draw and make it the County's finest chalk-carved feature.

over the surrounding land. Savour this spot before you continue, especially if you have excellent conditions and visibility on the occasion of your passage.

To continue the walk: head along the top of the horse to a **kissing gate** and, after passing through it, turn **R**. Now walk along the crest of the Downs that you have been admiring from the Horse. Passing a **trig point** – another, possibly even superior, lofty viewpoint – stroll along the Downs' edge until you almost reach a wooded area, and spy a **stile** uphill to your **L**. Head for this and cross it to join a lane that appears to double back on the route you have been following. Soon enough it straightens and very shortly leads to a **crossroads**. Take a **R** here and follow a **surfaced track** which, for a brief while only, is tree-lined. When the trees end, you will be aware of a dramatic quarry to your L and more stunning views to you R (north). This track is now a very welcome companion all the way to the outskirts of Upton Scudamore.

The views from this high belvedere are excellent all the way, first to the north and later to the west, where Cley Hill totally steals the show, its near perfect symmetry causing one to stop and admire, and contemplate a delightful ascent and lofty perch to come.

As you approach the village the lane descends and curves to the L. When you reach a **T-junction** turn **L**, and note the village sign ahead. Cross the **bridge** over the A350 to enter the village and head straight on, past the somewhat scruffy mini-suburbs, to the architectural delights to follow, as you approach **The Angel**, an upmarket pub with bar, restaurant and accommodation to match.

The Westbury Downs fall more than half-way between Wootton Rivers and Mere. However in many respects they represent a natural mid-way point. On a clear day, away to the east the curvaceous Pewsey Downs can be seen. In the same direction, but closer, Roundway Hill is prominent (these skyline treats enable you to admire almost your entire route so far) and, laid at one's feet, is an incredible swathe of Wiltshire countryside. But the ubiquitous Westbury chimney, now immediately ahead, offers a certain poignancy, in that it can be viewed from close to both ends of the walk and effectively, therefore, links the whole route, creating this sense of centrality.

The church of St. Mary in Upton Scudamore: a beautiful sight on approach from the village centre or quiet countryside to the south-west. On arrival it may well be open, enabling you to explore inside as well as out.

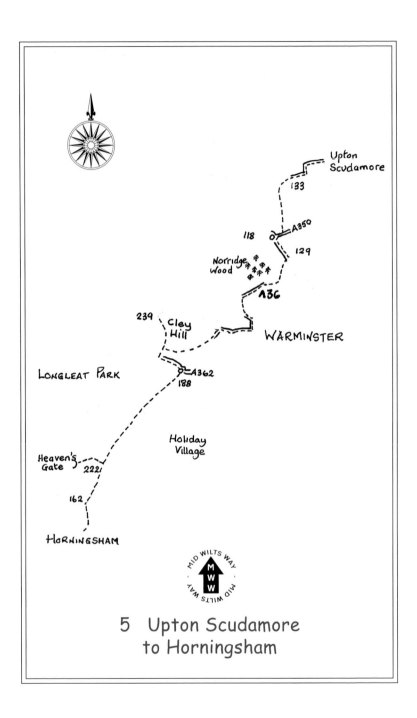

Upton
Scudamore

133

118 A350

129

Norridge
Wood

A36

239 Cley
Hill

WARMINSTER

LONGLEAT PARK

A362

188

Holiday
Village

Heaven's
Gate 222!

162

HORNINGSHAM

MID WILTS WAY
M
W
W
MID WILTS WAY

5 Upton Scudamore
to Horningsham

Stage 5: Upton Scudamore to Horningsham

Distance:	7.25m, 11km
Maps:	Landranger 183, Explorer 143
Accommodation:	Horningsham
Food and Drink:	Horningsham

The fields surrounding Upton Scudamore are especially pleasant and open, and before long the railway line is crossed on a quaint bridge, carpeted in grass. Soon the A350 is encountered and then, after more country walking, for a brief period the A36 is a necessary, though not particularly pleasant, companion. Once away from the road quiet countryside is rejoined and views of Cley Hill begin to dominate the scene.

Cley Hill is approached from the east and south, a slight disappointment as an ascent from the north would have been more aesthetically pleasing. Ironically, rights of way access all but a tiny stretch of the ground leading to the hill from the north, but the author could not secure written permission from the landowner to include this approach, thus the route described must suffice.

Views from the summit of the hill are glorious and will probably detain you for some time. Then a pleasant road walk leads through the Longleat Estate to the picture postcard village of Horningsham, the launch point for the final stage of the walk.

The **Angel Inn** is more or less in the centre of the village, and you pass it to the **R**, in effect heading straight on. You are now in the more attractive part of the village, with some beautiful cottages and luxurious houses to admire this way and that.

When you reach a **T-junction**, with the lovely little church to your L, turn **R** and stroll along the lane to a **stile** on the edge of the village. Cross the stile to enter an open and spacious field. Straight ahead of you, you will see a railway **bridge**; head for it and as you pass over it, note its carpet of grass – a pleasant, truly rural touch.

Turn immediately **L** and head for another little **bridge** in the distance. Cross it and head in the general direction of the A350/A36 **roundabout**. Soon you will cross another little **bridge** as you enter the final field before **crossing** the busy A350. This innocent looking stretch of land suffers from poor drainage and is sometimes home to boisterous young steers, so beware, it packs a hard punch! Joking aside, you will no doubt pass through it without incident.

Cross the A350 and take the **first exit** from the **roundabout**, signposted for **Warminster**. **Cross** the Warminster **road** and follow the **verge**, facing the oncoming traffic.

On the brow of the hill, turn **R** besides **Croft House Farm** (which offers B&B) into a lane and follow it to a **gate**, through which you turn **L** to pass through some trees, over a **stile** and into a field. Walking straight ahead you soon reach another **gate** into a second field. Once again head straight on to reach a **stile** leading to a wooded path. Very shortly this path curves **R** to emerge from the trees. You are now heading for the busy A36, but trees kindly obscure it at this stage.

Head beside the edge of a separate, larger wooded area, to reach a **stile** and then a **layby** on the A36. Turn **L** and follow the layby for just 0.3 miles, or about 5 minutes walking time. With Cley Hill ahead and to the R and another layby opposite, turn **L** and join a generous **track** to the fringes of Warminster. When the track reaches the **road** turn **R** following first the pavement and then the verge for a few minutes. Although the verge is narrow at first, the moment you step on to it, the turning off the road can be clearly seen ahead.

Turn **R** off the road with two adjacent tracks ahead of you, taking the **R** hand one to avoid the cattle grid. Pass under a road **bridge** and turn **L**. Shortly after, take a **R** to leave the road surface track via a stile. The countryside hereabouts is now gloriously open and the views of Cley Hill an interesting contrast with those previously enjoyed from a northern angle.

Pass through two fields, keeping to the field edges to pass over another **stile**. Now head straight on past an old, rather tumbledown shed. Shortly spy a **stile** on the **L**, cross it and drop down onto a wooded **path**. Continue in the same direction – west – to reach, in a few minutes, the **track** leading from the **National Trust car park** to **Cley Hill**.

To climb Cley Hill, turn **R** and follow the track to a **kissing gate** accompanied by interpretive signage. Please read the signs to ensure you ascend the hill by a route least likely to cause further erosion problems. Additionally, you might like to bear in mind the option of a complete circuit of the hill, which the Trust are keen to encourage. To do this, head around the base of the hill to the east and then north-west, keeping always within the perimeter fence. When you have walked beyond little Cley Hill, turn south to ascend it.

When, in moments, you reach the summit of this little outlier, stop to take in already superb views, including Cley Hill itself, now truly beginning to look like a small, grassy but steep mountain. Drop off the summit and then head steeply up onto Cley Hill proper, drinking in the incredible views and lofty sensation from both the trig point and higher ancient burial ground.

Having taken time to enjoy all aspects of this little hill, make your descent to the south-east to comply with the National Trust's wishes, avoiding the most eroded slopes. Then curve round to the **R** to reach the kissing gate once again. Pass through the gate and onto the access track, following it all the way to the **main road**, where you turn **L** onto the A362 to follow the verge with care, for less than five minutes, up to the **Longleat roundabout**. *Please note:* Though very brief, this is a potentially dangerous stretch of road. If you are walking with others, ensure you do so in single file and, when the verge narrows, consider crossing the road (again with care) to enjoy a wider verge and to face the oncoming traffic.

At the roundabout take the **second** of three possible **exits**, to join a wide, straight unclassified road, signposted to **Horningsham**. Continue along this road for a little over a mile, enjoying pleasant surroundings. As this road section draws to a close be especially careful because the road bends and twists briefly, simultaneously narrowing a little. Common sense should prevent incidents occurring but do be vigilant nevertheless. When you reach the purpose-built **car park** and trail out to the popular beauty spot of Heaven's Gate, the temptation to leave the MWW briefly and rejoin it in Horningsham may indeed be too great. However, I'm not at liberty to offer any instructions as this would contravene the wishes of the Estate.

Very shortly after the car park and trail, turn **R** onto a pleasant bridleway, following it downhill to a little **road**. Turn **L**, then soon after bear **L**, just as you reach a **phone box** (one of the red, old-fashioned variety). Note all around you the delightful, individualistic and scattered cottages, here on the fringes of **Horningsham**, and contemplate your journey so far, the end of another section and start of the grand finale still to come.

As this point conveniently marks the end of this section of the walk, you may be tempted to explore the village centre, which is just a few moments from the way itself. Your time will not be wasted as a range of delightful buildings await discovery and discrete investigation.

Cley Hill (pictured above) is, quite simply, a beautiful hill. Without doubt, the incredibly extensive panorama that awaits those who ascend it, is one of the finest on the whole of the walk. Viewed from many points in the surrounding countryside, its sudden and improbable steepness, lends it the form and character of a mountain in miniature. What is more, its relative narrowness on top ensures that the views in almost all directions are unimpeded. Only to the South, South-East do the trees of the Longleat Estate obscure the view.

Cley Hill is in the expert care of the National Trust, whose sensitive ownership and management of much of rural England is to be applauded loudly. Interestingly, in the summer cows are released to graze on the steep sided slopes, maintaining the close cropped appearance of this otherwise uncultivated hill of unique and shapely form.

Longleat is really the generic name for an enterprise that consists of the magnificent house, beautifully maintained parkland and forestry, the world's first 'Out of Africa' safari park and a host of other purpose-built attractions that blend with the landscape.

The house itself is a spectacular sight, both when experienced intimately via a detailed tour and when spied from the tops of the Deverills or, as seen above, viewed from Heaven's Gate. Opened in 1949 on a fully commercial basis, it was a trail blazer as many more stately homes soon followed Longleat's lead and opened their doors to fee-paying customers.

However, the safari park was arguably even more daring a move! In 1966 a hundred-acre lion reserve was opened to the public causing a furore of concern and interest. Within a year of opening, one million paying guests had flocked to see lions in a more natural habitat than any British zoo could hope to match, whilst in Parliament, questions were asked as to the safety of such a venture. Needless to say no lions, nor any other potentially dangerous animals (introduced later) have ever escaped from the park. With the passing of time, many more attractions have been seamlessly added, in an environment that appears permanently tranquil.

Sadly the MWW does not access the Estate, however you can shut your book and make your own way at this point, enjoying the informal access that has been tolerated by Estate managers for a long time. Perhaps the most sublime of all routes through the Estate, leaves the Cley Hill access track to the west, where the MWW joins it from the east, avoiding almost all road sections and taking in some of the most gorgeous scenery in the county.

Horningsham *boasts many historic buildings, thus the explorer is spoilt for choice. However, no visitor should miss the Congregational chapel, pictured below. Built in 1566, a staggering 123 years before the Toleration Act permitted such chapel congregations to meet legally, it is more than likely that its early years were marked by persecution and harassment for those in attendance. With a thatched roof, glorious setting and almost 450 years of history, there is ample justification for an extended visit.*

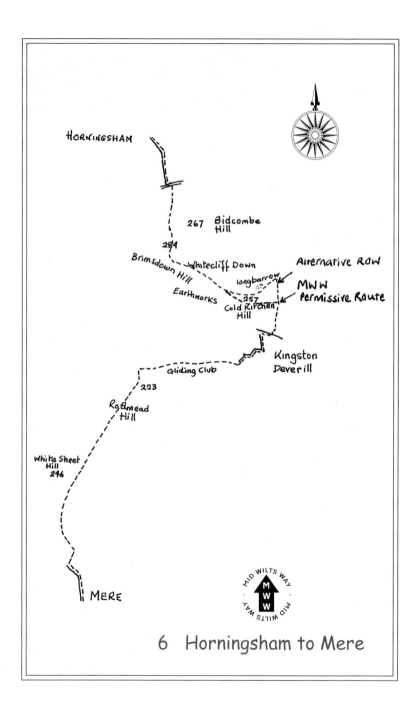

HORNINGSHAM

267 Bidcombe
Hill

284

Brimsdown Hill Whitecliff Down Alternative ROW

longbarrow MWW
Earthworks Permissive Route
257
Cold Kitchen
Hill

Kingston
Deverill

Gliding Club

223

Rodmead
Hill

White Sheet
Hill
246

MERE

6 Horningsham to Mere

Stage 6: Horningsham to Mere

Distance:	9m, 14km
Maps:	Landranger 183, Explorer 143
Accommodation:	Mere
Food and Drink:	Mere

Leaving Horningsham the route soon passes through some of the most open and undeveloped parts of the entire county, before heading up onto the lofty Deverill Downs. This makes for a fitting grand finale, being Wiltshire's second highest area of continuous high ground, second only, of course, to the Pewsey Downs over which the walk passed in Stages 1 & 2.

The Deverills offer outstanding views in every direction, and the access routes available ensure that walking is prolonged on their tops for as long as possible.

After dropping off the ridge to the charming village of Kingston Deverill, the route gradually ascends one final time to gain height and maintain it. As you pass over this peaceful landscape there is much to draw the eye, including the highest and separate Deverill ridge (see The Malverns of Wiltshire? page 71). However, nothing will prepare you for the final overwhelming vista that bursts into view when the hill tops offer their first glimpses of the Vale of Blackmoor. All of a sudden, a simply immense sweep of rural England is arrayed at your feet. To the east and south additional hills add a sense of scale to the scene but, if it is a clear day, it is the extraordinary horizontal panorama that will stop you in your tracks. Here you might view many possibilities for extending your route beyond Mere, or simply wish to stop and contemplate a stunning finish to a lovely walk.

As you descend the ridge narrows splendidly, offering airy views on both sides. Then, as you head into Mere, you will have lasting memories to ponder and perhaps a return or onward route to plan.

Continuing your journey from the end of Stage 5 in **Horningsham** (next to the old-fashioned public phone box to be precise), turn **R** at the next countryside junction and then immediately **L** at another signposted to **Longbridge Deverill**, Shearwater and Shaftesbury.

After just a few moments, as the road bends, turn **R** onto a bridleway **track**. Very soon you will be aware of just how remote a part of the county (and southern England for that matter) this area is.

When a quiet country **road** is reached, **cross** it and continue on another **bridleway** just very slightly to the **L**. Beyond the **gate** opening onto the bridleway trees briefly line the route, and even appear to hem you in against the fence to the R. Very shortly, however, all is open again as you start to climb onto the glorious Deverills – the roof of south-west Wiltshire. Just before you reach another **gate**, note a neat memorial stone to your L. This is a great spot from which to drink in the unspoilt rural tranquillity hereabouts.

Beyond the gate, the route enters a small **woodland**, following an **uphill track** right through its heart. In spring, glorious bluebells carpet the ground to your R and L adding yet more diversity and colour to this lovely walk. The path levels out on the top of this broad Deverill ridge and then starts to descend a touch as a **gate** is reached, leading out of the woods. Straight ahead, a **ridge-top fence** is clearly visible; head straight for it to continue the walk.

However, if you turn R immediately after the aforementioned gate a track leads swiftly back into and then out of the trees, after which a few steps to your R lead to a glorious view over the Longleat Estate.

To continue the route: when the **fence** is reached, keep it to your R and **follow the ridge** east-south-east. This is another part of the walk to be savoured to the full.

Similar to other elevated sections of the MWW, this ridge-top passage is nevertheless unique in that slopes fall on both sides to distant valleys, and the views in all directions, near and far, are dramatic, incredibly rural and quite different to those previously enjoyed and experienced.

Shortly pass through a **gate** (probably open), after which the ridge begins to rise again. After passing a large hill-top beacon, the official right of way bears L away from the fence to ascend Cold Kitchen Hill, over cultivated ground. However, to stay on the MWW do not follow this route. Instead keep to the **fence** and follow it – enjoying continuously good views to the R and straight ahead – until you reach a little **gate**, at **trig point** 849 38 (OS Explorer map 143).

This short, permissive path was very carefully negotiated with the landowner, to avoid potential damage to crops, any navigational problems and a sizeable partridge shoot. I cannot stress strongly enough that the landowner concerned was of a very generous and positive spirit and thus this permissive alternative should be utilised and simultaneously respected.

After passing through the **gate**, head south, over the ridge's extended whaleback, soon reaching another **gate** and **stile**.

Now head downhill to a field **fence** and **gate**. Straight ahead and downhill again, another **gate** marks the foot of the ridge and leads onto a **lane** where the way turns to the **R**. In a few moments a **junction** is reached where you turn **L**. Then, just before you reach the main **road junction**, turn **R**, immediately after the delightful **Bell House**, an architectural gem and the prelude to an exquisite passage through Kingston Deverill, one of the Way's most remarkable villages.

Now well and truly in the heart of the penultimate village on the MWW, you will no doubt note how this incredibly peaceful and sleepy little settlement drips with chocolate box charm, and thus every step through it should be enjoyed to the full. A rich variety of cottages - thatched, simple, colourful, small, large, old, modern but in a vernacular style - may prove to be a considerable distraction, causing you to look every way except straight ahead!

At a small **junction**, take a **L** (in effect straight on) beside **River Cottage**, noting also the presence of the infant Wylye river to your R. Continue along the lane taking a **R turn** as it bends back on itself. After a short while turn **L** and pass immediately through a **gate** into a small field. Now head straight on to pass through a much smaller **gate** on the other side of the field. The gate leads onto a **track** which you cross to pass through another **gate**, leading into open countryside once again. Continue on a gentle uphill gradient with the **fence** to your immediate L.

As you approach some trees and a gate, an end-on view of the highest and separate Deverill ridge will no doubt draw your eye. Particularly dramatic from this angle, this broken ridge increasingly looks like a scaled down version of the Malverns. However, you will not find these slopes invaded as is the case with their larger counterparts some way to the north; on the contrary, if you decide on a detour to explore them intimately, you will almost certainly have them to yourself.

Continue with the **fence** to your **L** and look out for gliders; on a plateau to your L, the launch and landing sight add another interesting feature to this final stage.

When you reach a **cross-fence** turn **L** and pass through a **gate**, heading now in a southerly direction. Soon the path becomes fenced on both sides, at which point you turn **R** through another **gate**. Walk across the field in a south-westerly direction to reach another **gate** and then continue straight ahead with the **fence** to your **R**. Continue in a south-west-south direction without deviation, passing through **three gates** to reach a prominent track in about a mile. Cross the **track** and pass through yet another **gate** to head straight on but also in the direction of a **fence** to your **R**. This narrow stretch of open access land leads to your final descent on the MWW into Mere.

Suddenly, these high, flat-topped hills fall slightly, then narrow into a remarkable ridge, offering an amazing view of the Vale of Blackmore – a huge expanse of lowland, rural bliss.

This is such a fitting finish to the MWW and you may just recall how it all started in a village beneath the towering slopes of the Pewsey Downs. Here too Mere sits beneath steep hills and in rural surroundings, despoiled only by the passage of the A303.

Stay on the ever narrowing **ridge** as it descends and then follow a **track** to the **L** beneath its gradually falling crest. This track becomes stony and then bends to the R. Stay on this track all the way to the **lane/road** at the foot of the hills where, beside a house. you turn **L**.

Follow the road over the A303 via a **bridge**, and continue all the way into the village. When the village centre is reached, spy straight ahead the **Angel Corner Café** just across the road. This is a truly fitting establishment in which to celebrate and/ or mourn your journey's end.

Dear reader, if just a fraction of the pleasure I have experienced walking the MWW has been yours too, you will have had a richly rewarding journey, and will no doubt, be eager to walk more long distance routes both within the region and, perhaps, further afield.

Mere: your final destination after a cross-county walk of 55 miles

The Malverns of Wiltshire?
Ascending gently from Kingston Deverill, your gaze will most probably be held by an end on view of the separate and highest Deverill ridge. Away to the West, this ridge, sliced in two by the B3092, rises so impressively from the surrounding flat landscape that it may well remind you of the Malvern Hills. Of much smaller scale in every sense, it nevertheless rises improbably, enticing one to seriously contemplate a diversion to take in the ridge. Access from the B3092 is tricky, making an approach from the MWW perhaps, intriguingly, the most viable option.

Are these hills the Malverns of Wiltshire?

The Deverills

The Deverill Hills are a lovely series of wide yet long ridges in the delightfully quiet south-west corner of the county. Rising to almost 1,000 feet above sea level, they offer diverse and wide-ranging views of rural landscapes that appear almost remote. Similar in height to the Pewsey Downs, they provide a dramatic climax to the route when walking in a southerly direction. However, they are also distinctly different from the Pewsey Downs, in that the ridges are not as continuous, and have been farmed more extensively too.

As a point of significant interest, when on the highest Deverill top the route crosses, the distinctive chimney beneath Westbury White Horse can be seen way to the north east, thus visually linking almost the entire MWW.

A fitting climax to the Mid-Wilts Way: the Mere Downs where they drop steeply, just to the north of the village

Tourist Information Centres (TICs)

There are a good number of TICs covering the Mid-Wilts Way, therefore I have simply listed them, along with telephone numbers and the villages for which they have accommodation listings. Such accommodation information is prone to go out of date quickly, so a village with limited options may, at some point in the future, cease to be listed, should accommodation providers close up and/or move on and no new providers emerge. That said, the TIC staff will always be best placed to update you.

Two providers of accommodation passed *en route* are individually listed; the White Hart pub in Oare and Croft House Farm, just off the A350/A36 roundabout. This is because, in the case of the former, the pub is not listed with any TIC but provides a strategically important option and, concerning the latter, because the farm is somewhat isolated and thus when planning, walkers would not necessarily be aware of its existence and location, though, again, it occupies a strategically important spot.

Devizes TIC: for Wootton Rivers to Devizes; Tel. 01380 734669

Calne TIC: for Calstone Wellington; Tel. 01249 814000

Trowbridge TIC: for Steeple Ashton; Tel. 01225 710535

Warminster TIC: for Upton Scudamore, Corsley and Horningsham; Tel. 01985 218548

Mere TIC: Tel. 01747 861211

Specific options *en route*

Oare: The White Hart; Tel: 01672 562273 (not registered with any TIC)

A350/A36 Roundabout: Croft House Farm; Tel: 01985 213460 (Availability is variable so plan with care if considering this option)

Scenery so typical of the MWW

Suggested itineraries

Itineraries are a very personal affair. That said, a range of options and ideas can always help to make the planning stage a more enjoyable and trouble-free activity. What follows are tentative suggestions for walking the route in a variety of ways. This is not to say some people would not wish to stake out an entirely different plan; no doubt many will, but the itineraries included here are perhaps likely to be amongst the most logical and popular.

Two days

If trying to complete the MWW in two days you'll have to hurry, and day two will demand an early start along with steely determination. That said, in good conditions and if time is severely limited, it can be done. You'll need to get to Steeple Ashton on day one (approximately 30 miles), a worthy objective, but a considerable undertaking. Then on day two, despite having less miles to cover, you'll probably not want to overdo your breakfast and, resisting the considerable charms of the village, you will need to make a purposeful start, keeping one eye firmly on your watch.

Three days

In every way my favourite option, and perhaps the most logical when attempting to combine good progress with enjoyment, as well as sensible start times on days two and three.

You'll need to get to Devizes on day one, but after quite a long and satisfying day you'll be able to relax a little, enjoying (on day two) a good breakfast before pulling on your boots for some more miles ahead. You will then need to aim for Upton Scudamore or perhaps Croft House Farm (close to the outskirts of Warminster and just off the A350/A36 roundabout). Then, after another relaxed start on day three, you should comfortably reach Mere in time for some afternoon tea.

Four days

If planning to walk the route in four days you have some interesting options to consider.

Unless you live in the region, you may well arrive in Pewsey by train, still some way from the start. You could take a bus to Oare, check in at the White Hart pub and then complete a lovely, half-day, part-circular walk, by following the MWW east to Wootton Rivers and then returning to the Pewsey Downs via lanes and roads. On day two you could head for Devizes with its good range of accommodation and services. On day three Upton Scudamore could be your objective, leaving day four to complete the rest of the walk.

Alternatively, you could start conventionally in Wootton Rivers and head for Morgan's Hill, leaving the way to the north to overnight in Calstone Wellington.

On day two you could then set out for the delightful village of Steeple Ashton, perhaps the nicest place *en route* to rest your weary head and legs. On day three you could set your sights on Corsley or Horningsham, the latter another gorgeous village, leaving day four for a relaxed and delightful finish as you stroll down from the Deverills into Mere.

Six separate day walks covering the route in both directions
For those living in the area, this type of itinerary does have some advantages, not least that you can be fully independent, returning to your starting point at the end of the day, and you get to cover the route in both directions, building in a few variations if you so desire.

Stage 1 is especially well suited to such a venture. When you reach the Wansdyke path you could follow it eastwards back to the Knapp Hill car park. Then approaching Oare, instead of dropping off the Downs you could stay high and follow a track curving south on high ground to reach your outward path just east of where the ridge plunges down to the lane on the outskirts of Oare. Such a route (circular of sorts) would enable you to approach the Pewsey Downs from the east, in my view one of the most stunning prospects anywhere on the MWW.

Stage 2 presents limited opportunities for any variation on return, but you do get to walk the dyke in both directions! What more encouragement do you need? You could of course turn back at Roundway Hill, saving your legs and some more climbing on your return journey. But you then have to live with not quite completing all of the way, or walking a little further next time. You no doubt will have noticed that starting out precisely from Tan Hill is not possible, however you could start at the Knapp Hill car park and head north-west to join the dyke, or you could start in Devizes instead and make Tan Hill your turning point.

Stage 3 would require an out-and-back canal stretch, which might not be so appealing to some. That said, you would get to see Caen Hill in both directions, and you could vary the route by following the White Horse Trail from Keevil to the canal via Bulkington and Poulshott.

Stage 4 works especially well as an out-and-back, especially as the prospect of lunch at the Angel might spur you on. But do be careful not to eat too much as there's an immediate after-lunch ascent to get you back up onto the Downs. If you have reservations about following the road from Dunge to Bratton, you could try it one way and the White Horse Trail the other, placing you in the best possible position to reach an informed view.

Stage 5 is lovely but you will have to make some tough decisions. Will you close your guidebook (figuratively speaking) and select from a delightful range of options through the Longleat Estate or will you follow the inferior, but official, roadside path? The choice is yours.

Stage 6 is magnificently suited to an out-and-back trek. The stunning scenery is gorgeous in both directions. Kingston Deverill falls about half way and thus provides a lovely place to stop and rest for a while and both Horningsham and Mere are delightful locations with facilities available too. Even if you walk the MWW conventionally, as a continuous multi-day affair, don't dismiss the possibility of returning to complete this section on the basis here described.

What options! Surely for all long distance walkers planning the adventure is a significant part of the overall experience; may it be so for you. I sincerely hope you enjoy both the planning and execution of the walk and, you never know, we might even pass one another on the way. Happy planning and walking!

Acknowledgements

I would like to thank Dot Williams, Richard Broadhead and Allan Francis (all of Wiltshire County Council), Chris Boyes, Anthony Julyan and Dr. Robert Oliver for the initial and ongoing encouragement they provided concerning plans for a guidebook to the Mid-Wilts Way. Thanks also to Joan Alsop (my sister-in-law) for the excellent sketch maps and Susan Hewitt who reviewed an early draft of the guide, offering candid and supportive feedback, and who continued to encourage me to seek publication.

I also want to thank my wife Kate, whose tolerance and kindness enabled her eccentric husband to complete the draft over a short, but intense period of time.

Finally, special thanks to the publisher and editor, Roger Jones, without whose help the finished product would never have been produced in so professional and timely a manner.

About the Author

 James Alsop has been a keen walker for the past ten years, having climbed nearly half the Scottish Munros, several Welsh peaks and a number of mountains on the island of Mallorca. However, of late, his focus has increasingly turned to lowland, coastal and moorland walking, especially in the south-west of England, where the combination of coast and countryside has largely captured his affections for the outdoors.

James lectures in Tourism, Business and Politics at Wiltshire College. He is married to Kate and they have two daughters, Evangeline and Isabella.

More books on Wiltshire subjects from Ex Libris Press:

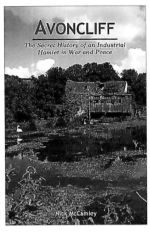

AVONCLIFF:
The Secret History of an Industrial Hamlet in War and Peace

by Nick McCamley

A thoroughly researched, entertainingly written and truly fascinating account of this dimunutive Wiltshire community situated on the River Avon, Kennet & Avon Canal and Railway between Bradford on Avon and Bath.

ISBN 1 903341 23 X
208 pages; £9.95

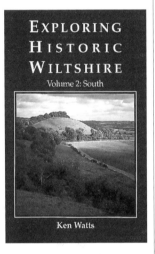

EXPLORING HISTORIC WILTSHIRE
Volume 2: South

by Ken Watts

Featuring six of the finest landscapes of rural south Wiltshire. Includes a series of guided walks.

ISBN 0 948578 92 0
176 pages; £7.95

Volume 2: North reprinting in Autumn 2007

HIDDEN DEPTHS:
Wiltshire's Geology and Landscapes

by Isobel Geddes

Shows how the country's hidden depths are the basis of the landscape we see on the surface. A detailed introduction to Wiltshire's geology and the only book on the subject currently available.

ISBN 0 948578 05 1
224 pages; £9.95

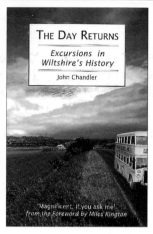

THE DAY RETURNS

by John Chandler

The perfect dipping into book for all lovers of Wiltshire, packed with arcane facts, stories and characters, presented in an entertaining and accessible way.

ISBN 0 948578 95 5
256 pages; £7.95

THE MARLBOROUGH DOWNS

by Ken Watts

The only book on the most accessible chalk downland in the county. Full of fascinating background. Includes a series of guided walks.

New edition
ISBN 0 903341 15 9
192 pages; £9.95

WHERE WILTSHIRE MEETS SOMERSET
20 Best Walks in the Country around Bath, Bradford on Avon, Trowbridge, Westbury, Warminster and Frome

by Roger Jones

A bestseller since 1982!

New revised edition
ISBN 1 903341 34 5
128 pages; £6.95

All the above titles are available via your local bookshop or from EX LIBRIS at 1 The Shambles, Bradford on Avon, Wiltshire, BA15 1JS. Tel 01225 863595

EX LIBRIS PRESS, 16A St John's Road, St Helier, Jersey, JE3 2LD. Tel 01534 780488
E-mail: roger.jones@ex-librisbooks.co.uk   www.ex-librisboooks.co.uk